VIENNA
THE CITY AT A GLANCE

CW00734068

Franziskanerkirche
Located a stone's throw from the
shopping streets of Graben and K
is this striking church, overlookin
cobbled square. To appreciate it in full,
stop for a drink at Kleines Café (see p045).
Franziskanerplatz

Stadtpark
Built in 1862, this delightful park is perfect
for an evening stroll. Don't miss the
Otto Wagner-designed Stadtpark U-Bahn.

Stephansdom
This Gothic marvel towers above the ancient
streets of Innere Stadt. Building began in
1304 and the church's continued presence
after sieges, bombardments and WWII
is nothing short of miraculous.
Stephansplatz

Innere Stadt
This warren of cobbled medieval streets
has the highest concentration of attractions
for visitors. It's possibly the quietest
and most enjoyable city centre in Europe.

MAK
The Museum of Applied Arts has an impressive
permanent collection, a surprisingly good
design shop and the excellent Österreicher
im MAK café/restaurant (see p041).
See p036

Café Prückel
Opened in 1903, this Viennese *Kaffeehaus*
is a convenient stop for a little post-MAK or
post-Stadtpark refreshment.
Stubenring 24, T 512 6115

INTRODUCTION
THE CHANGING FACE OF THE URBAN SCENE

Situated at the crossroads of central Europe, beneath the foothills of the Alps, Vienna has what estate agents like to call location, location, location. One of the original multicultural capitals, the city boasts an enviable wealth of intellectual and artistic pursuits. Though once a large and revered capital that ruled over a vast and powerful empire, Vienna began to look unwieldy and anachronistic when the country's borders shrank to the present-day mountainous buffer between Germany and Italy. Even now, many Austrians regard their fellow countrymen, the Viennese, as being effete, élitist and unnecessarily cultured.

Since Austria joined the European Union in 1995, Vienna has looked at ever expanding and culturally diverse Europe with fresh, if still slightly nervous, eyes. Yet visitors who arrive today will be aware of a growing self-confidence. In the Innere Stadt, they will find an easy-going and relatively compact city centre, packed with stunning attractions that bear witness to Vienna's rich artistic and architectural history. Venture out from here and, making use of an almost embarrassingly effective public transport system, the city's famous parks, the art hub that is the Museumsquartier, its *Kaffeehäuser* and a growing number of impressive new bars and restaurants are all within easy reach. And, should all this culture prove too much, a multitude of tempting out-of-town destinations are literally on the city's doorstep.

ESSENTIAL INFO

FACTS, FIGURES AND USEFUL ADDRESSES

TOURIST OFFICE
Wien Tourismus
Albertinaplatz 1
T 24 555
www.vienna.info

TRANSPORT
Car hire
Avis
T 587 6241
Hertz
T 512 8677
Metro
U-Bahn
www.wienerlinien.at
Taxis
Taxi 31 300
T 31 300
www.taxi31300.at
Taxi 60 160
T 60 160
www.taxi60160.at

EMERGENCY SERVICES
Ambulance
T 144
Fire
T 122
Police
T 133
24-hour pharmacy
T 1550

EMBASSIES
British Embassy
Jauresgasse 12
T 716 130
www.britishembassy.at
US Embassy
Boltzmanngasse 16
T 313 390
www.usembassy.at

MONEY
American Express
Kärntner Straße 21-23
T 5124 0040
travel.americanexpress.com

POSTAL SERVICES
Post Office
Fleischmarkt 19
T 0577 677/1010
Shipping
UPS
T 0810 006 630
www.ups.com

BOOKS
**On Architecture (Studies in Austrian
Literature, Culture and Thought)** by
Adolf Loos and Daniel Opel (Ariadne Press)
The Third Man by Graham Greene (Penguin)

WEBSITES
Architecture
www.azw.at
Art/Design
www.designaustria.at
Newspapers
www.diepresse.at
www.derstandard.at

COST OF LIVING
**Taxi from Schwechat International
Airport to city centre**
£32
Cappuccino
£2.30
Packet of cigarettes
£3.10
Daily newspaper
£0.95
Bottle of champagne
£85

VIENNA
Area
415 sq km
Population
1.8 million
Currency: euro
€1 = £0.77 = $1.55
Telephone codes
Austria: 43
Vienna: 1
Time
GMT +1

Prague
Basel
Vienna
AUSTRIA
Milan

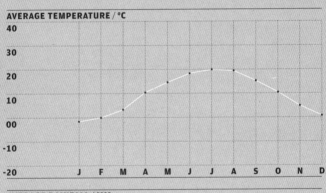

AVERAGE TEMPERATURE / °C

40												
30												
20												
10												
00												
-10												
-20	J	F	M	A	M	J	J	A	S	O	N	D

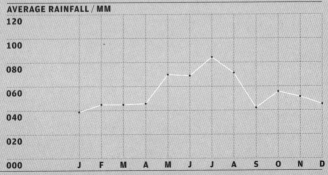

AVERAGE RAINFALL / MM

120												
100												
080												
060												
040												
020												
000	J	F	M	A	M	J	J	A	S	O	N	D

NEIGHBOURHOODS
THE AREAS YOU NEED TO KNOW AND WHY

To help you navigate the city, we've chosen the most interesting districts (see below and the map inside the back cover) and colour-coded our featured venues, according to their location; those venues that are outside these areas are not coloured.

DONAUSTADT

A few metro stops to the north-east of the city centre lies Vienna's answer to Canary Wharf. Squeezed on an isthmus of land between the new and the old Danube, the area contains 1,500 dwellings, impressive skyscrapers and the eye-grabbing Vienna International Centre (see p010), one of the United Nations' four headquarters. Danube City is a modern interpretation of Vienna's social planning schemes of the 1920s.

LEOPOLDSTADT

Vienna's second district, named following the expulsion of the Jews by Emperor Leopold I, is experiencing a change in fortune. Infamous at one time for being poverty stricken, the area is now gaining attention because of the proposed U2 metro extension, and gentrification has well and truly started. To the east, Prater park is famous for *The Third Man* icon, Riesenrad (www.wienerriesenrad.com).

MUSEUMSQUARTIER

This 60,000 sq m cultural district, housed in a former riding stables, is one of the success stories of contemporary Vienna. Austrian architects Ortner & Ortner fused the old with daring new builds, such as MUMOK (Museumsplatz 1, T 52 500) and the Leopold Museum (see p032), to create a much-needed urban focal point for both the Viennese and tourists. Less successful is the Quartier21 area, which tries too hard for the design-savvy visitor's attention.

FREIHAUSVIERTEL

This small triangle between Karlsplatz, Wiedner Haupstraße and Rechte Wienzeile is an alternative shopper's paradise. One of Vienna's most unappealing areas until recently, it is rapidly becoming a boutique and design-shop haven (though many of the original shopfronts and fin-de-siècle apartment entrances are still to be found). The focus is on Schleifmühlgasse, a small street with a stencil by graffiti artist Banksy.

NEUBAU AND SPITTELBERG

The seventh district is a real hotchpotch of residential streets, modern high-street chains, hippy shops and some of Vienna's most avant-garde stores, such as Park (see p076). Spittelberg's narrow, cobbled streets were once a working-class, artisanal quarter, but they are now gentrified and pedestrianised, and home to cafés such as Das Möbel (see p074) and Vienna's traditional corner pubs (*Beisls*).

INNERE STADT

Today's Innere Stadt roughly translates as the limits of the medieval city, which later became the domain of dukes, princes and ambassadors. Now this World Heritage Site is a mix of baroque and modernist buildings centred around the city's august Gothic cathedral, Stephansdom. Unlike most inner-city districts, it's a surprisingly peaceful area to explore on foot, where exclusive shops and boutiques mingle with bars, restaurants and cobbled squares.

LANDMARKS

THE SHAPE OF THE CITY SKYLINE

No other European city's history is as visible as Vienna's, and a canny visitor will spot the clues everywhere: from the Roman and Habsburg city limits delineated by today's Ringstraße to the wider boundary of the Gürtel and the ring of railway arches that set Otto Wagner on course with Austrian modernism. Many of Wagner's ideas stemmed from his time with the artists of the Vienna Secession, but it was his Österreichische Postsparkasse (see p012) that fired one of the first shots against classical architecture. The development of social housing also helped to mould today's city. It was Wagner's student, Karl Ehn, who designed the Karl-Marx-Hof (Heiligenstädter Straße 82-92), the defining symbol of *Rotes Wien*, or Red Vienna, the municipal socialist era.

The 1970s saw the building of Danube City, the business and residential hub squeezed onto a small piece of land between the new and old Danube. With the construction of the vast UN bureaucratic beehive, the Vienna International Centre (see p010), the city stepped forward onto the world stage from a design point of view. Many of Europe's most prominent architects – Zaha Hadid, Hans Hollein, Günther Domenig and Jean Nouvel – have reinforced this presence. With future projects such as Dominique Perrault's DC Towers, the Monte Laa housing development and TownTown (www.towntown.info), this trend is set to continue.

For full addresses, see Resources.

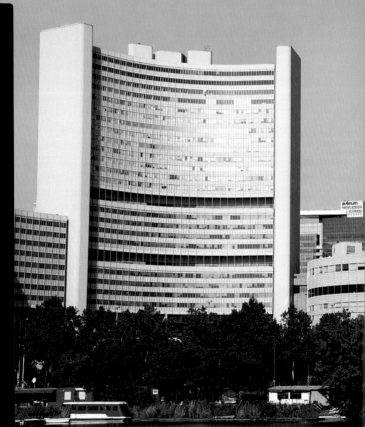

Vienna International Centre

This trefoil-shaped collection of office blocks in Donaustadt is representative of Austria's desire to be at the heart of modern Europe. Housing one of the UN's four seats and the International Atomic Energy Agency, it was designed by Johann Staber. Six 110m curved slabs fan out from a cylindrical conference centre. *Wagramer Straße 5, T 26 060, www.unvienna.org*

Österreichische Postsparkasse

After all these years, Otto Wagner's Postal Savings Bank is still striking and still strikingly beautiful. In 1903, he won a competition for a new-concept build that would mirror the bank's new, innovative procedures. In contrast to the quasi-imperial palaces of the other entrants, Wagner's eight-storey brick structure featured a thin Sterzing marble skin, studded with aluminium. Inside, the main hall rises up to a curved, frosted-glass ceiling, pierced by its supportive iron columns, while the floor consists of ultra-thick glass blocks, allowing light to flood in to the administrative heart below. There's a small Wagner museum (T 53 453) on site.

Georg-Coch-Platz 2, www.ottowagner.com

Transformer Station

Although industrial brutalism might not be the leading style associated with Vienna's architectural past, this modernist transformer station in the 10th district should form part of any serious architour of the city. Completed in 1931 for Wien Energie, the concrete and brick electricity-generating substation is one of the best-known projects by Eugen Kastner and Fritz Waage. Making excellent use of its limited, triangular site, the functionalist design bears more than a passing resemblance to a battleship, featuring portholes, a long 'bridge' and an imposing, curved 'prow'.
Humboldtgasse 1-5

T-Center

This building sparked the redevelopment of the former St Marx abattoir and cattle-shed complex in the Landstraße area. Designed by Austrian architects Günther Domenig, Hermann Eisenköck and Herfried Peyker, T-Mobile's headquarters won the State Prize for Architecture in 2006. The 60m-high structure, 255m long with a 40m cantilevered wing, resembles a reclining skyscraper. With 134,000 sq m of useable floor space, it's the largest private building project in Austria. And while it looks like an expressive leap away from Olbrich and Wagner, the symbolism for its client (an innovative company, now collected under one roof) is similar to that of the Österreichische Postsparkasse (see p012). Other developments earmarked for the area include a transparent office building and an extension of the Media Quarter Marx development.
97-99 Rennweg

HOTELS
WHERE TO STAY AND WHICH ROOMS TO BOOK

As you would expect, Vienna contains some of the most plush and historic hotels in Europe. It also has a vibrant design-hotel scene. But actually finding a room in a city with so many attractions is not that easy, so don't bank on bagging your first choice when booking a last-minute weekend break, especially during spring, summer and Christmas – though prices do tend to drop in July and August due to the annual city-wide opera vacation. Four hotels – institutions really – stand out: the operatic Hotel Bristol (see p022); Hotel Imperial's stately residence (Kärntner Ring 16, T 501 100); the former rakes' playground of Hotel Sacher Wien (Philharmonikerstraße 4, T 514 560); and finally the Palais Coburg (opposite), which is heavy with Saxe-Coburg history, features a sumptuous décor and offers first-class service.

It's on the boutique front that the modern accommodation story really begins. Terence Conran's first foray into hotel design was Das Triest (Wiedner Hauptstraße 12, T 589 180), and many hotels that came afterwards make more than a passing reference to this trendsetter. Smaller places, such as the sumptuous Altstadt (see p020), the novel Hotel Rathaus Wein & Design (see p028) and the Hollmann Beletage (Köllnerhofgasse 6, T 961 1960), have an idiosyncratic charm, while slick newbie, the Do & Co Hotel (see p031) has raised the benchmark for larger establishments.
For full addresses and room rates, see Resources.

Palais Coburg

Some buildings are born great, others are the result of having greatness thrust upon them. Fewer, like the Palais Coburg, are both. Built in 1845 by the Duke Ferdinand of Saxe-Coburg and Gotha, the palace was saved from neglect by Peter Pühringer in 2003. Thirty-five of the suites are named after a Saxe-Coburg blue blood, such as the Victoria Imperial Blue (above), which hides its technology amid regal styling.

More contemporary rooms include the open-plan, Japanese-influenced Modern Suite. Elsewhere, guests will find part of the medieval city wall in the Stadtbild room (overleaf), which leads to the largest private wine cellar in Europe, a Michelin-starred restaurant (see p038) and, best of all, a rooftop pool, which is often empty. *Coburgbastei 4, T 518 180, www.palais-coburg.com*

Stadtbild room, Palais Coburg

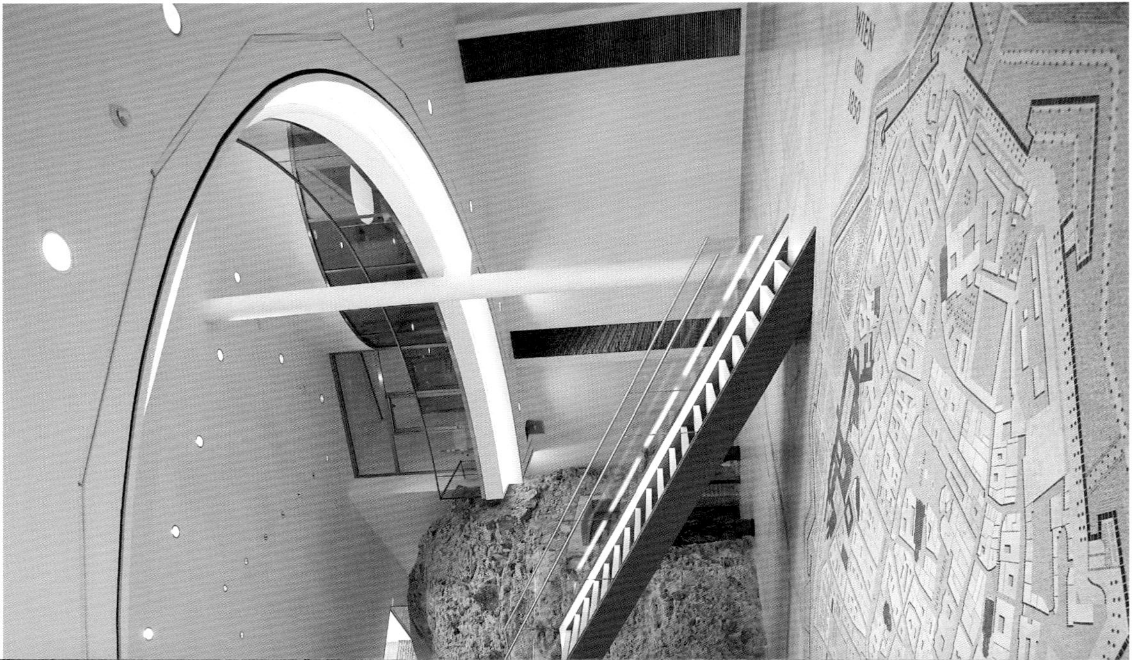
WIEN
1850

Altstadt

The word decadence springs to mind when surveying the nine Matteo Thun-designed rooms in this lovely 49-room *Gründerzeit* pension. Finished in June 2006, along with the opulent hallway, they recall the frivolous life of Vienna's most famous courtesan, Josephine Mutzenbacher. Dark-oak parquet floors and damask wallpaper contrast with white Catalano basins and chandeliers from Prague. The Matteo Thun Suite, also known as the Master's Chamber (above and right), panders to the muted erotic, with Helmut Newton books scattered about, dark striped wallpaper, cognac-coloured soft furnishings and a black Bisazza mosaic and glass-door shower. The money shot here, though, has to be the central freestanding bath set on its own polished platform.
Kirchengasse 41, T 522 6666, www.altstadt.at

Hotel Bristol
Music and opera play a key role at the
Bristol, where visitors have ranged from
Joan Baez to Enrico Caruso. The imposing
lobby of this landmark, opposite the
Staatsoper (T 51 444), belies the quiet
fin-de-siècle charm of its rooms. Reserve
the Prince of Wales Suite (pictured) and
dine in the hotel's exquisite restaurant.
Kärntner Ring 1, T 515 160,
www.westin.com/bristol

Le Méridien

This vast, 294-room hotel is a short stroll from the Museumsquartier, but mainly appeals to business travellers and Middle Eastern tourists. Yvonne Golds (of Real Studios, London) used light and art installations to bring this imperial apartment block up to date. The main lobby, inspired by the city's theatrical history, places permanent pieces beside a revolving display of local, contemporary video and performance showcases. The in-house bar and restaurant are elegant places to wine and dine, while the pool (above) in the fitness area is a stylish place to take a dip. Many of the rooms here (right) are let down by veneered furniture, but it's the bathrooms, with Philippe Starck's Axor fittings, multi-jet Pharo showers and heated mirrors, that are the real draw.

Opernring 13, T 588 900,
www.lemeridien.com

The Levante Parliament
Named for its proximity to the Austrian
legislature, what was once a Bauhaus-
inspired turn-of-the-century medical
clinic was recast in May 2006 as a swish
74-room bolthole that will appeal to both
buttoned-up bureaucrats and Vienna's
beau monde. Austrian architect Michael
Stepanek paid homage to the building's
modernist origins by marrying Turkish
marble and dark mahogany, favoured
materials of the Vienna School, with light
stone and glass, such as in the Junior
Suite (above) and the lobby (right). In fact,
glass, especially as art, is a central theme
at the Levante, thanks to Romanian artist
Ioan Nemtoi's eponymous restaurant/bar
(T 228 2860), which features his dramatic
hand-cut pieces. The cuisine on offer is
east meets west, and is created by local
chef Elisabeth Strunz.
Auerspergstraße 15, T 535 4515,
www.thelevante.com

Hotel Rathaus Wein & Design
Opened in 2004, this 33-room relative
newcomer to the Viennese boutique-hotel
scene, situated in the western eighth
district, hits all the right notes. Each of
the modern, stylish rooms, such as Room
404 (right), boasts walnut flooring, rain
showers and a scattering of original
fin-de-siècle tiling, and is dedicated to
an Austrian vintner, while the minibar
comes stocked with the best of the range.
The hotel is spread over four floors of
an historic townhouse, each evocatively,
if erratically, serviced by an original
wrought-iron cage lift. The hotel's director,
Martina Pöll, a wine academic, keeps the
marble bar stocked with more than 300
Austrian wines, such as Gesellmann's
spicy Blaufränkisch Hochacker and the
Joseph Pöckl Zweigelt. The bar serves a
buffet breakfast and snacks in the evening.
Lange Gasse 13, T 400 1122,
www.hotel-rathaus-wien.at

Style Hotel

This former *Jugendstil* (art nouveau) bank was given the Maria Vafiadis touch in 2003. With transparency a dominant theme, this hotel feels bigger than its 78 rooms would suggest. The lobby (above), with its muted colours and velvet drapes, appeals to pinstriped city types. Vafiadis wanted to recall the elegance of the 1920s, but her choice of dark woods, and brown, orange and red upholstery and tiling, feels more mid-20th century. The rooms are generous in their size and facilities, and have good bathrooms as well as a scattering of Josef Hoffmann-inspired furniture. To add to the hotel's mix, there is an Italian-inspired restaurant, Sapori, and a popular bar, H12. *Herrengasse 12, T 227 800, www.stylehotel.at*

Do & Co Hotel

Amsterdam-based interior design firm FG Stijl has created a delicately sumptuous 43-room hotel, owned by Do & Co, in the upper echelons of Hans Hollein's iconic Haas House. The rooms feature deep sofas, suede padded walls and teak floors, which complement the louvred teak modesty-shutters of the glassed-in rain showers. Try to reserve one of the suites, such as Suite 400 (above), which come with their own private onyx bars and stunning views of Stephansdom; the 10 rooms without a view of the cathedral offer huge jacuzzis with inlaid plasma screens by way of compensation. This attention to detail extends to the hotel's Onyx Bar (see p042) and the in-house restaurant, where an Asian-inspired menu is served in ultra-modern surroundings.
Stephansplatz 12, T 24 188, www.doco.com

24 HOURS

SEE THE BEST OF VIENNA IN JUST ONE DAY

Attempting to draw up a list of things to do in 24 hours in Vienna is a thankless, Sisyphean task. Just when you think you have a definitive itinerary, you have to start again as another must-see hoves into view. Conveniently, many of the city's attractions are clustered in or close to Innere Stadt. If not, the metro and five-line tram system provide a super-efficient service.

Leaving aside the wedding-cake excess of the Hofburg Palace (Michaelerplatz 1, T 533 7570) and the musical heritage for which Vienna is rightly famed, the city has a dizzying choice of excellent museums, any of which, such as the Kunsthistorisches Museum (Maria-Theresien-Platz, T 5252 4591), is a draw in itself. And it's with a museum that we recommend you start your day. But first get yourself a Vienna Card (€18.50), a 72-hour pass that gives you unlimited use of public transport and discounted museum entry.

After breakfast at 'UNA' (opposite), head to Museumsquartier and specifically the Leopold Museum (Museumsplatz 1; T 525 700). From here, it's a short walk to the Kunsthalle Wien Project Space (Treitlstraße 2, T 587 0073). Stop off at the café, one of the hippest lunch spots in town, before visiting MAK (see p036) and dropping into the Schullin jewellery store (see p037). End your day at Restaurant Coburg (see p038), where the fine wines will help you forget you haven't even begun to scratch the city's cultural surface. *For full addresses, see Resources.*

9.00 Café-Restaurant 'UNA'

Designed by Paris-based architects Anne Lacaton and Jean-Philippe Vassal, 'UNA' is part of the Az W (or Architekturzentrum Wien) museum (T 522 3115). The venue's stated desire 'to employ elements that stem from another part of the world' was perfectly realised with furnishings by Stephan Seehof and Hussl Möbel and tiles from Istanbul. The vaulted ceiling, with its geometric shapes and patterns, is reminiscent of a Turkish hammam. The dominant theme, of the building process itself, can be noted in the unplastered walls and simple lighting. Thanks to friendly staff and an imaginative menu, 'UNA' is deservedly popular, so arrive early. Afterwards, wander through to the museum, which explores 20th-century architecture in chronological order. *Museumsplatz 1, T 523 6566, www.azw.at*

12.30 Kunsthalle Wien
The next destination is a renowned institute for contemporary art, now housed in a functional, industrial-style building by Ortner & Ortner near the Winter Riding School. Its previous home, a temporary structure on Karlsplatz by Adolf Krischanitz, has been turned into the Kunsthalle Wien Project Space.
Museumsplatz 1 T 52 18 90,
www.kunsthallewien.at

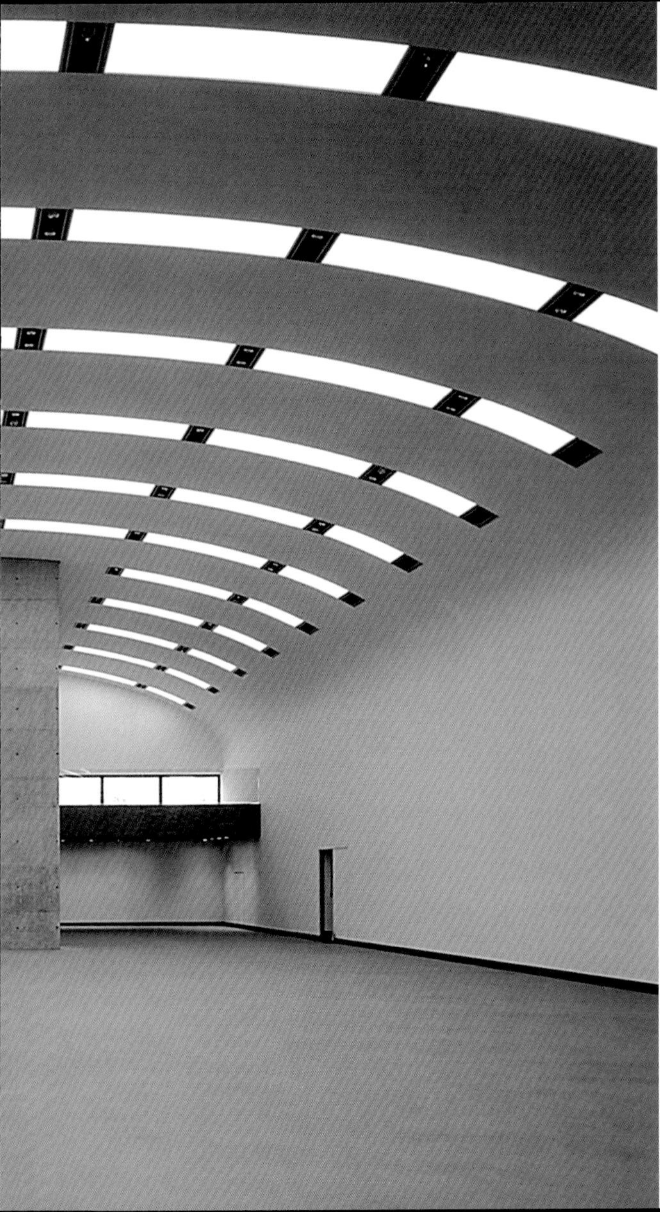

15.00 MAK

The Museum of Applied Arts (known as MAK), built in 1871 by Heinrich von Ferstel and inspired by London's V&A Museum, should be on the itinerary of every visitor. Inside, the designers were given a blank canvas. In the Jugendstil Rooms, Barbara Bloom created shadow screens to show the evolution of chair design through silhouettes, and within the Baroque Room you'll find the tiny Porcelain Room, which was painstakingly rebuilt after being removed piece by piece from the Palais Dubsky in the Czech Republic. Alongside this are a contemporary art exhibition space (above), a shop selling works by local designers, and the acclaimed café Österreicher im MAK (see p041).
Stubenring 5, T 711 3060, www.mak.at

17.00 Schullin

After a look around the MAK, head for the Schullin jewellery store (above) on Kolmarkt. Designed by Hans Hollein in 1981, the shop's façade, with its striking bronze arc, has proved just as much a draw for architourists as Hollein's design for the former Schullin store (now owned by Caesar's) located on nearby Graben. Completed a decade earlier, this boasts a blue marble façade punctured by a dramatic Dalí-esque ravine of rolled gold, creating what must be one of the city's most dramatic entranceways – worth a visit even if you don't step inside.
Kolmarkt 7, T 533 9007, www.schullin.at

21.30 Restaurant Coburg

This Michelin-starred dining room is housed within the luxurious opulence of the Palais Coburg (see p017) and the interior vies with the menu for your attention. Chef Christian Petz, formerly of Julius Meinl am Graben (see p072), reimagines classic dishes – order the cheeks of veal with leek and semolina dumplings. The wine list is excellent too.
Coburgbastei 4, T 518 180, www.coburg.at

URBAN LIFE
CAFÉS, RESTAURANTS, BARS AND NIGHTCLUBS

Viennese nightlife and cuisine have always revealed a profusion of outside influences. Traditional dishes include a hearty mix of Eastern European carbohydrates and meats, Italian pasta, and spices from Hungary and further east, while recently, the city's *junge und wilde* (young and wild) chefs and restaurateurs have become known for a willingness to take risks, casting their culinary nets a little further, to Asia. Most menus now have a stir-fry or sushi section and some, such as those at Österreicher im MAK (opposite), successfully fuse oriental and Austrian dishes. This fresh approach to Viennese cooking is mirrored in the design of many eateries, and is led by architects such as Eichinger oder Knechtl (Österreicher im MAK; Palmenhaus, Burggarten, T 533 1033) and BEHF (Yellow, see p046; Fabios, see p059; Yume, Bergmillergasse 3, T 416 9267).

Music has always been central to the cultural life of Vienna, and today, classical concert programmes featuring the works of Haydn, Schubert, Beethoven and Strauss can be enjoyed alongside sets by modern-day mix-meisters Kruder & Dorfmeister, who have made electronica and house a prominent part of the city's live music scene. You'll find the best clubs peppered throughout Innere Stadt, by the banks of the Danube Canal and along the Gürtel, and a small cluster of good bars located around Nussdorfer Straße and Josefstädter Straße underground stations.

For full addresses, see Resources.

Österreicher im MAK

Über-cool local architects Eichinger oder Knechtl turned their attention to the MAK (see p036) café in 2006. Renamed Österreicher im MAK after the arrival of culinary hero Helmut Österreicher from Steirereck im Stadtpark (see p044), the traditional Austrian pub/restaurant formula has been given a visual shot in the arm here. Dramatic ceilings and smoked-oak parquet flooring are married with minimalist booths and there's a glass *Extrazimmer* (extra room), complete with retractable roof. There are two tempting menus on offer, a traditional one and a more modern version, both featuring dishes that rely heavily on local ingredients. We prefer the latter, which features dishes such as catfish with stewed peppers.
Stubenring 5, T 714 0121,
www.oesterreicherimmak.at

Onyx Bar
Six floors up this Hans Hollein landmark,
looking out of curved-glass windows over
Stephansdom, is the Onyx Bar, within the
Do & Co Hotel (see p031). Arrive around
10pm, when cocktails are served to a
youngish crowd across a backlit onyx
bar. Turkish damask chairs, arabesque
tables and teak flooring add visual
spice, while the music is upbeat house.
Stephansplatz 12, T 24 188, www.doco.com

Steirereck im Stadtpark

One of Vienna's most exclusive eateries opened at its new address in 2005, in one of the city's former *Meierei* (a milk market allowing city dwellers to buy direct from the dairy farmer). The Reitbauer family's restaurant reflects their twin fascinations: their Styrian origins and Vienna's theatrical history. The designers, Art for Art, mixed baroque gold furniture with handmade mirror-backed red tiles in The Ess Bar on the ground floor, while the for-hire dining space upstairs is all velvet drapes and Murano chandeliers. The hip Meierei bar on the lower ground floor is more casual. The well-chosen menu mirrors the opulent surroundings, and the 150-item cheese board, the extensive wine list and the cigar sommelier will have you back for act two. *Am Heumarkt 2a, T 713 3168, www.steirereck.at*

Kleines Café

During the 1970s, most developments in the city were put in the hands of large commercial practices, but a few chose to think small. Designed by architect Hermann Czech, this diminutive café/bar (as the name suggests) is owned by one of Austria's best-known actors, Hanno Pöschl. Czech, who also refurbished the Immervoll restaurant (T 513 5288), as well as creating a footbridge in Stadtpark, looked to the nearby Loos American Bar (see p050) for some style pointers. Like Adolf Loos, he used mirrors to improve a claustrophobic interior, and the simple exterior of the Kleines Café echoes the designs of the early 20th century. Located on the edge of a quiet, cobbled square, this is a charming place to stop for a coffee or a drink.
Franziskanerplatz 3

Yellow

Opposite Vienna's Westbahnhof station lies the Asian eaterie Yellow. Ahron Hu enlisted the talents of architects BEHF to design every aspect of the restaurant, right down to the takeaway packaging. The yellow dining area represents day and the black bar, night. Try the black pepper tiger shrimps.
Mariahilfer Straße 127, T 595 1155, www.yellow.co.at

Weingut-Christ

Visiting a *Heuriger* (wine tavern) is a must here. Vienna's northern districts boast great conditions for wine growing, and it's a centuries-old tradition for small producers to invite locals to taste their new wine. Most *Heurigen* are rustic and somewhat kitschy throwbacks to the 'good old days', but Weingut-Christ has been hauled into the present day by Rupert Königswieser and Ferenc Horvath of design team Raum-Werk-Stadt, with the use of natural stone, timber and brushed aluminium. Visitors need not fear spying a single pair of lederhosen. Open Tuesdays and Wednesdays every other month from January (3pm to 9pm; €15 per person). *Amtsstraße 10-14, T 292 5152, www.weingut-christ.at*

Loos American Bar
This dark, diminutive bar was designed by
Adolf Loos in 1908. Mirrors are carefully
placed to create the illusion of space,
while Loos' distaste for ornamentation
and fondness for natural materials are
evident. The English-speaking staff mix a
perfect dry martini, and a jazz soundtrack
adds to the intimate atmosphere.
Kärntner Durchgang 10, T 512 3283,
www.loosbar.at

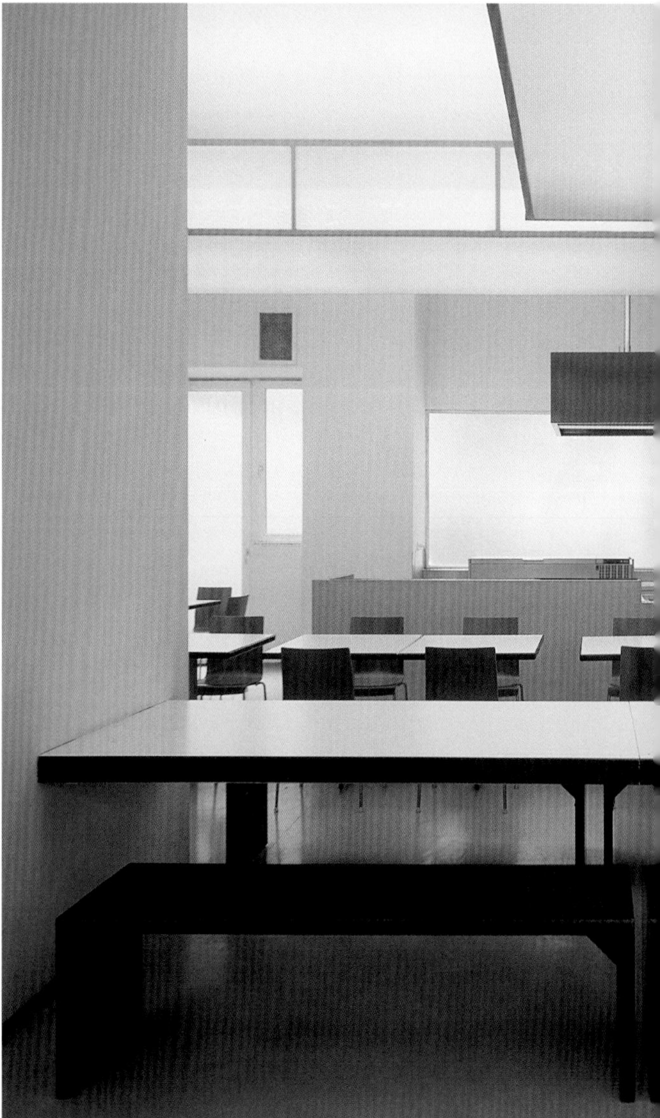

Ra'Mien
This minimal noodle restaurant run by
Chinese artist Yang Tie offers a soup-
heavy Chinese, Japanese and Vietnamese
menu. Downstairs, in a small bar/club
awash with chaises longues and mirrors
depicting dragons and cherry blossom,
local trance and progressive house
DJ Acan often makes an appearance.
*Gumpendorfer Straße 9, T 585 4798,
www.ramien.at*

Volksgarten

The Volksgarten, in the heart of the city
directly by the Hofburg, is really three
clubs in one. The recently renovated
Clubdiskothek room, which you access
through the Winter Garden (right), is
home to the glamorous weekly Garden
Club (think Roger Sanchez and Ibiza
favourites Pacha, Space and Circoloco),
and now has a retractable roof. This
night, run since 2001, has become the
stomping ground of models, starlets
and VIPs. Also in the Volksgarten is the
500-capacity Evergreen Garden (closed
in winter), which has a cocktail bar and
amphitheatre. The third option is the
Kortische Säulenhalle (commonly known
as The Banana), a summer pavilion built
by Oswald Haerdtl in 1958 as a temporary
structure. Featuring Günter Ferdinand
Ris-like chandeliers, it hosts a weekly
night popular with a young crowd.
Burgring 1, T 532 4241, www.volksgarten.at

Shambala Bar
Interior designer Yvonne Golds achieved stunning results at Le Méridien hotel's (see p024) Shambala Bar with her clever use of lighting. The recessed 'catwalk' lights lead the eye to illuminated niches. Also on display are video installations and, on club nights held in spring, the work of local graphic artists.
Opernring 13, T 588 900,
www.lemeridien.com/vienna

Planter's Club

If you're seeking a respite from concrete, glass and steel, this colonial-style cocktail bar is worth a visit. Latticed mahogany doors, worn leather armchairs, potted palms and a lazily turning ceiling fan that blows cigar smoke around conjure up the atmosphere of an ex-pat club. But it's the drinks that people come here for, as there are more than 800 whiskies and 350 rums on offer. Competent staff offer advice, before heading up to the library-style spirit gallery to hunt for that 1885 St James' Martinique Speciale rum. At €200 for a 4cl measure, it will be worth the wait.
Zelinkagasse 4, T 533 339 315, www.plantersclub.at

Fabios

Conceived by architects Armin Ebner and Markus Spiegelfeld of BEHF, Fabios is owned by Fabio Giacobello, and was the winner of the Loos Architecture Prize 2003. It has become something of an institution among Vienna's smart set, who are attracted by its classy American walnut floors and ceilings, and chocolate leather sofas. The bar's extensive Austrian and Italian wine list is accompanied by cocktails that tend to be low on alcohol but high on taste, such as the Fabolose Aperativ (prosecco with orange and raspberry). The restaurant is housed in a glass-front extension, where chef Christoph Brunnhuber focuses on Italian fish dishes, such as carpaccio of smoked swordfish from Lipari with tomatoes and Sicilian olive oil.

Tuchlauben 6, T 532 2222, www.fabios.at

Passage
Vienna's newest super-club is a fairly
sterile and sparsely furnished space
with a touch of *Solaris* about it, where
lighting delivers the main impact.
Owned by Sunshine Enterprises, it has
seen the likes of local vinyl kings Kruder
& Dorfmeister guest-appearing as well as
other big names of the Europe DJ scene.
Burgring/Babenbergerstraße, T 961
8800, www.sunshine.at

INSIDER'S GUIDE

FELIX MUHRHOFER, KITCHEN DESIGNER

Felix Muhrhofer set up design store Cuka (Naglergasse 21, T 699 2280 4040, www.cuka.at), which specialises in modular kitchen systems, and also runs a cooking club at the shop. He starts the day at The Breakfastclub (Schleifmühlgasse 12-14), an easy-going café where après-clubbers and early birds set themselves up for the day. For lunch, you'll find him at Noi (opposite, Payergasse 12, T 403 1347), near the Brunnenmarkt food market, where they prepare delicious Mediterranean-influenced dishes. Muhrhofer also recommends Die Schöne Perle (Grosse Pfarrgasse 2, T 0664 243 3593) for its traditional cuisine.

A favourite stop for coffee is Crupi (Margaretenstraße 3, T 0664 391 0667), where the owner sells produce made by his family in Sicily. For dinner, Muhrhofer heads to Gasthaus am Nordpol 3 (Nordwestbahnstraße 17, T 333 5824), where the Czech owner, a Slovakian chef and Vietnamese twins serve Russian food. On a night out, Muhrhofer often begins at the bar in the Austrian Film Museum (Augustiner Straße 1, T 533 7054) in the Albertina. The venue is repainted each month to reflect the retrospective on show. Then he heads to Loos American Bar (see p050), but not until 2am, when barman Roberto has time to explain the philosophy behind his Roberto Special. Muhrhofer ends the night at Kafe Shabu (Rotensterngasse 8, T 460 2441), which is famed for its absinthe. *For full addresses, see Resources.*

ARCHITOUR

A GUIDE TO VIENNA'S ICONIC BUILDINGS

A cursory glance through many a travel guide would have the uninitiated believe Vienna is a conservative maze of sepia-stained cobbled streets and baroque mansions. While there are certainly sufficient examples to keep picture postcard-style photographers happy, this image hides the city's progressive nature. Adolf Loos' Steiner House (St Veit-Gasse 10) is worth a visit to witness the experiments that were taking place in home design 100 years ago, which soon became the norm throughout Europe. And even though it initially caused controversy, Hans Hollein's now iconic Haas House (Stephansplatz 12, www.hollein.com) shows an admirable desire to take chances, given its location opposite Vienna's defining tourist attraction, the Stephansdom (Stephansplatz).

The *Gemeindebauten* social-housing schemes of the interwar years haven't escaped reinvention in the late Harry Seidler's Hochhaus Neue Donau (opposite) and nearby Wohnpark Neue Donau projects. Old gas containers weren't seen as too daunting a structure for reinterpretation either, as the Gasometer (see p068) city-within-a-city testifies. Even churches didn't escape the urge of modernism, and although Christus Hoffnung der Welt (see p066) and Church of the Most Holy Trinity (see p070) are very different, they represent the same hunger for fresh ideas – an impressive feat in any city, let alone one with such a wealth of traditions. *For full addresses, see Resources.*

Hochhaus Neue Donau

Finished in 2001, the 32-storey, 150m-high Hochhaus Neue Donau is the tallest residential building in Vienna. Harry Seidler's structure was constructed using reinforced concrete and a metal-clad façade, while the triangular footprint of the tower is intended to maximise views of the Danube. The vertical core connects the two housing wings, which contain 373 apartments, with a seven-storey office wing. Hochhaus Neue Donau is seen as a figurehead for Seidler's nearby Wohnpark Neue Donau social-housing project, which was completed in 1998. Despite his early minimalist origins, which the Austrian-born architect honed in his adopted country of Australia, this work shows an inclination to use the latest technology to produce highly expressive finishes.
Wagramer Straße, www.seidler.net.au

Christus Hoffnung der Welt
The initial impression of Heinz Tesar's
church is of a stark, black, chromium-
steel-plated cube, but he performed
a miracle with this building. It appears
much larger inside, as daylight floods the
birch plywood interior and, after dark,
light bursts out like a beacon from the
portholes and a deep cut in the ceiling.
Donaucitystraße 2, T 263 0952,
www.donaucitykirche.at

Gasometer

Four former gas containers, built in 1896, have been renovated to within an inch of their lives in Simmering. Decommissioned in 1984, the complex, nicknamed 'G-town', now contains offices, shops, cinemas and apartments. Each of the towers, known as Gasometer A, B, C and D, is constructed in two-tone red brick and stands 75m high. Four architects were given a tower each: Jean Nouvel created an indoor plaza with translucent roof, and Coop Himmelb(l)au added a 22-storey building to the existing tower (above and left). While there's still something slightly sinister about G-town, a post-apocalyptic city where *Judge Dredd* meets *Blade Runner*, Manfred Wehdorn's eco-friendly, terraced Gasometer D, with its indoor garden, is very accessible. *Guglgasse 8-14, T 748 4800, www.wiener-gasometer.at*

Church of the Most Holy Trinity
Out in the 23rd district of Liesing, where
the city of Vienna meets Vienna Woods,
lies the only architectural statement
by sculptor Fritz Wotruba. Completed in
1976, it consists of 152 concrete blocks
separated by narrow vertical glass panes.
The apparent chaos of the asymmetrical
blocks is intended to create a harmonious
whole once you enter, where a surprisingly
large space provides a peaceful place
for worship. It's a more chaotic version of
Kisho Kurokawa's Nakagin Capsule Tower
in Tokyo, finished a few years earlier. The
church can accommodate 250 people and
caused a storm of protests when it was
first built, but its setting, composition and
materials make it a powerful building that
exhibits the expressive flourish which can
be seen throughout Vienna's history.
Rysergasse/Georgsgasse
T 888 5003, www.georgenberg.at

SHOPPING

THE BEST RETAIL THERAPY AND WHAT TO BUY

While it's unlikely you would visit Vienna solely for its shopping, the city's compactness, cobbled lanes, burgeoning boutique scene and good transport links make it an attractive retail destination, even for those used to Milan's finest shops. There are few large department stores or malls, but the central Ringstrassen-Galerien (Kärntner Ring 5-7, T 512 5181) is one fashion arcade of note, housing Interio and Sir Anthony. High-end international chains cluster around Kohlmarkt and Graben, as well as local institution, the aristocratic food merchant Julius Meinl am Graben (Graben 19, T 532 3334). An important area to explore for antique furniture from the Wiener Werkstätte is Spittelberg. Specialist stores, such as Rauminhalt (see p086), can be found in Schleifmühlgasse in particular.

Many shops retain their elegant fin-de-siècle shopfronts, though some have been lost in the past two decades with the ubiquitous global branding of Mariahilfer Straße and Kärntnerstrasse. But retail architecture is back in vogue, helped by projects such as Hans Hollein's Haas Haus. Nowhere is this more apparent than in the designer boutiques of Neubau, like the Belgian-focused Park (see p076), bespoke opticians Brillen.manufaktur (see p085) and, most surprisingly of all, the BEHF-designed Tiberius (Lindengasse 2, T 522 0474), one of Europe's most exclusive and stylish sex stores, which should brighten any shopping trip.

For full addresses, see Resources.

Lobmeyr

For glassware collectors, Lobmeyr's 150-year-old store on Kärntnerstraße is an essential destination. This exquisite wine decanter (above), price on request, with black enamel *broncit* detailing, was designed by Josef Hoffmann in 1912 and is part of the designer's 'Serie B' set, which is held in the permanent collection at MoMA in New York. Inside Lobmeyr, you'll also find the Wiener Glasmuseum, a small exhibition showing pieces the company has been crafting since 1823. And should you buy this lovely object, don't, whatever you do, hide it away in your drinks cabinet when you get home. *Kärntnerstraße 26, T 512 0508, www.lobmeyr.at*

Das Möbel
Since 1998, Das Möbel has combined
a gallery, a coffee house and a product
showroom. Every six months a brand-
new range of furniture, from mostly
contemporary European makers, is
placed in the café, so you can try before
you buy. Many of the designs on sale
in the shop make playful use of space.
Burggasse 10, T 524 9497,
www.dasmoebal.at

Park

Sandwiched between the mainstream shops of Mariahilfer Straße and the drippy-hippy incense outlets of Neubaugasse is the large 480 sq m Park. Owned by fashion lecturer Markus Strasser and Helmut Ruthner, the shop sells designer and streetwear fashion, plus a limited selection of footwear, art books and perfumes. Their aim was to keep the shop itself in the background, presenting the clothes in an open space, and much of the store's décor can be moved, allowing the setting to be used for presentations and fashion shows. Park showcases work by European designers, with Belgians figuring highly. For women, check out Veronique Branquinho's modern but classic blazer (€650) and, for men, the individual and influential Raf Simons' plastic-covered fleece hoodie (€325).
Mondscheingasse 20, T 526 4414, www.park.co.at

Das Kunst Werk

Wolfgang Roth and Harald Steininger share a passion for 20th-century design and launched Das Kunst Werk in 1996 from their 260 sq m Laimgrubengasse shop. As well as the works of the Wiener Werkstätte, such as Josef Hoffman, Otto Wagner and Adolf Loos' furniture from 1900 to the 1930s, the duo searches out the tubular steel objects of Bauhaus designers, like Marcel Breuer, and Russian art deco. In 2000, they opened a smaller outlet on Operngasse, which focuses on rare Murano glass objects and iridescent Lötz vases. Our favourite pieces were the perfectly restored bentwood chairs by Michael Thonet and J&J Kohn, priced from €400 to €3,000.

Laimgrubengasse 24, T 650 230 9999;
Operngasse 20, T 650 230 9994,
www.daskunstwerk.at

Song

Owned by South Korean Myung-Il Song, this chic 500 sq m shop specialising in avant-garde fashion was designed by Gregor Eichinger (one half of architects Eichinger oder Knechtl). The conventionally styled entrance area belies the industrial, unrefined feel of the shop's interior, which features Annelies Oberdanner wallpaper and a Franz Graf table. The large space at the back of the store is flooded with natural light from the glass roof and is perfect for parading in the latest pieces by Walter van Beirendonck, AF Vandevorst and Bernhard Willhelm. There's a room dedicated to Martin Margiela, designed by Maison Margiela Interieur-Architects. *Praterstraße 11-13, T 532 2858, www.song.at*

Woka

Woka's owner Wolfgang Karolinsky has collected the casting moulds and press tools from the Wiener Werkstätte and, with the consent of the founding designers' families, makes handmade reproductions of pieces by Loos, Moser and Hoffmann. All items, such as Moser's 'Reininghaus' (above), a 1903 table lamp in brass or nickel, €1,779, come with an authentication stamp and a certificate filled in by the individual craftsman. There is also an impressive range of products by designers such as Hans Hollein, Walter Schmögner and Christian Ludwig Attersee. *Palais Breuner, Singer Straße 16, T 513 2912, www.woka.com*

Unger und Klein
A visit to this temple to viniculture
should be on every wine buff's wish list,
as it has a simple solution for those
disinclined to buy wine before tasting it.
Specialising in Austrian wines, Helmuth
Unger sells by the glass in the rear. If it
tantalises your taste buds, you'll find it
on the sleekly curved shelves out front.
*Gölsdorfgasse 2, T 532 1323,
www.ungerundklein.at*

Michél Mayer

This small boutique is located near the upmarket shopping areas of Graben and Kohlmarkt. Michaela Mayer's two-room premises is the nerve centre of her operation. As is de rigueur in high-end Viennese retail outlets, the shop is featureless white, save the (exposed) light fittings, brushed aluminium and dark timber flooring. The long, thin salesroom, really no more than a walkway, leads to the workshop/design studio. Designed by Sandra Häuplik, it opened in 2001 with minimal signage. Mayer's 2006 collection concentrates on dresses and skirts in soft, flowing silk and fine chiffon, with unexpected detailing. The men's collection includes traditionally cut, casual pieces in beige and brown. *Singer Straße 7, T 967 4055, www.michelmayer.at*

Brillen.manufaktur

Hidden away in Neubau, Vienna's seventh district, is this small store selling glasses, and, by a spatial sleight of hand, Brillen. manufaktur manages to pack a lot in. The shop-length display cabinet doubles up as the main storage unit. Since opening in 2002, it has added an on-site optician, and now designs its own products and is happy to accept one-off commissions. The owner, Nikolaus Hauser, eschews labels such as Gucci and Armani in favour of Theo, LA Eyeworks and Alain Mikli.
Neubaugasse 18, T 523 8200,
www.brillenmanufaktur.at

Rauminhalt
Close to Vienna's design heart are
Antiquitäten, or upmarket antique
stores, specialising in furniture.
A struggling fur outlet until the 1990s,
this 120 sq m store now displays work
by Charles and Ray Eames and Carl
Auböck (among others) as well as
Moroccan Berber carpets.
Schleifmühlgasse 13, T 409 9892,
www.rauminhalt.com

SPORTS AND SPAS

WORK OUT, CHILL OUT OR JUST WATCH

Given the Austrians' penchant for carbohydrate-rich meals and their famed sweet tooth, you'd be excused for thinking that their trim physiques were down to a miracle. Truth be told, the Viennese are very active and outdoorsy. The main reason is the sheer choice of sporting activities available to them throughout the year. Hot summers and a famously pristine environment mean swimming and sailing on the Danube are enormously popular, while cooler days see many heading for the nearby Wienerwald (Vienna Woods) for a spot of walking or cycling. And, unlike in the UK, active types don't hibernate just because winter has arrived; many pack their walking poles or skis and take to the Alps.

Vienna's cycle lanes make hopping on a bike an ideal way to see the sights. Citybike Wien (www.citybikewien.at) hires out cycles which you drop off at any one of their 50 stations around the city. For gym fiends, Holmes Place (Wipplingerstraße 30, T 533 979 090) is a plush option, while John Harris Fitness am Margaretenplatz (Strobachgasse 7-9, T 544 1212) boasts a futuristic new centre and medical spa. Amalienbad (see p092) should not be missed for its striking architecture and mosaic interior, while those with a head for heights should check out Kletterwand am Flakturm climbing wall (Esterhazypark, T 585 4748), where a 30m scale is all that's between you and a stunning view of the city's skyline.

For full addresses, see Resources.

Sacher Spa

Once infamous for its rich *Sachertorte*, Hotel Sacher is now known for having the best spa in the city. Visitors are spoilt for choice by an impressive range of facilities and treatments, from an aroma-salt steam room, massage and waxing services to the luxurious sauna (above). Packages range from €180 to €400 and use products by La Prairie and plant extracts by Ligne St Barth. We were tempted by the chocolate treatments, such as the enticingly titled Symphony In Chocolate, €180. And you thought it just tasted great.
Philharmonikerstraße 4, T 514 560; www.sacher.com

Krieau

In 1913, Emile Hoppe, Marcel Kammerer and Otto Schonthal designed Europe's first steel and concrete grandstand for the Krieau harness racetrack (the second oldest track in Europe after the Moscow Hippodrome). They were Otto Wagner's star pupils at the Akademie in Vienna and collaborated with him after graduation before setting up their own firm. The Krieau is a protected historical monument and was restored in 2002 to its pre-war glory. In summer, the arena is used as an open-air cinema. *Nordportalstraße 247, T 728 0046, www.krieau.at*

Amalienbad

When this public bath opened in 1926, it was one of the largest in Europe, and caused local dignitary Franz Siegel to opine that it was 'a symbol of the rise of the working classes to a new culture'. And indeed it did set a new standard for public buildings of the time. With room for 1,300 bathers, sun lamps, a sauna, terraces, a towel service and a beautiful mosaic interior, it gave the working population their first taste of luxury. Designed by Karl Schmalhofer and Otto Nadel, the curved glass roof opened at one time, flooding the 33m-long main pool with sunlight. The rather austere exterior, with its grandiose clock tower (also a water tank), hides one of the most stunning places to swim. There are single-sex bathing times or get in touch with your inner European and go mixed; it's €4 for a swim or €12.50 with a sauna. *Reumannplatz 23, T 607 4747*

Ernst Happel Stadion
Designed by Otto Ernst Schweizer and
completed in 1931, the Prater Stadium
hosted the International Worker's
Olympics held that year. After some
remodelling, it was renamed in 1992,
after the famous Austrian footballer and
manager. Now the stadium is used for
rock concerts, swimming championships
and it will stage the Euro 2008 Final.
Meiereistraße, T 728 0854

ESCAPES

WHERE TO GO IF YOU WANT TO LEAVE TOWN

With so much to see in Vienna, there really should be no need to leave its 23 districts, but those keen to take advantage of its central European location will find it very easy to escape to the nearby cities of Prague, Budapest, Venice or Ljubljana. With the CAT high-speed train (www.cityairporttrain.at) from Wien Mitte station to Schwechat International Airport taking only 16 minutes (every half hour, €9 single), short-haul flights are hassle free. Luggage can even be checked in at the train station. For a more leisurely sortie, boat trips with DDSG (www.ddsg-blue-danube.at) on the Danube to Budapest (€79) or Passau (from €117.50) are unbeatable.

Staying within Austria's borders, day trips are possible to the Wienerwald, which stretches from the city's outer districts all the way to the Alps. Langenlois (opposite) is famous for its wine, while adrenaline-lovers should head west to the sports capital of Innsbruck, where the ancient city centre and spectacular Tyrolean mountain scenery vie for attention. There's year-round snow on the Stubai Glacier, making summer skiing breaks possible. Graz, the UNESCO World Heritage city and Styrian capital, is only 40 minutes away by plane and is famed for its cafés, cuisine and otherworldly Kunsthaus (see po98). The surrounding countryside is home to the bizarre hotel/spa Rogner-Bad Blumau (see p102), the brainchild of self-taught architect Friedensreich Hundertwasser. *For full addresses, see Resources.*

Langenlois

An hour from Vienna and minutes from the charming town of Krems and the UNESCO World Cultural Heritage site of the Wachau, Langenlois makes a good base from which to explore. It is the largest wine-growing town in Austria, and the vineyard of Weingut Fred Loimer (T 02734 2239) deserves more than a lightning visit. American architect Steven Holl designed the spectacular 82-room Loisium Hotel, as well as the vineyard's brushed-aluminium visitors' centre (above). The hotel lobby is bedecked with Franz Wittmann furniture, while the dark tones of the Wine Library have a muted feel. Relax with one of the wine and spa treatments on offer, and be sure to try out the futuristic steam room.
Loisium Allee 2, T 02734 77100, www.loisiumhotel.at

Kunsthaus, Graz

Two hours south of Vienna is the UNESCO World Heritage city of Graz, which is worth a trip if only to see the Friendly Alien, designed by Peter Cook and Colin Fournier. A black box of tricks allows the structure's light-studded skin (known as the BIX Façade) to become a canvas for exhibitions held there.
Lendkai 1, T 0316 8017 9200,
www.kunsthausgraz.at

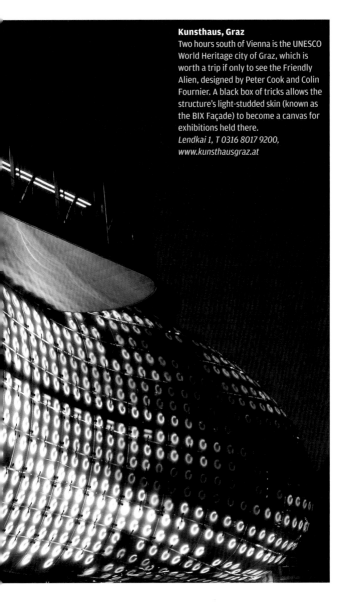

Mavida, Zell am See

The spa and winter ski resort of Zell am See, near Salzburg, makes for a convenient Vienna escape. In summer, the mineral-water quality of Lake Zell is enticing, while the surrounding 2,700m alpine peaks, with winter skiing on Kaprun Glacier, ensure active adventures. Architect Niki Szilagyi designed the Mavida, where inside you'll find inviting brown-leather seating islands and rich textiles chosen to complement those of British designer Tricia Guild. The 47 rooms are large and feature minimalist pieces by Casamilano. They also have excellent balcony views. After your sporting pursuits, have a drink on the Terrasse (above), a massage, or unwind in the flotation tank or Blue Box multi-sensory relaxation room. *Kirchenweg 11, T 06542 5410, www.mavida.at*

Rogner-Bad Blumau, Bad Blumau
Environmentalist and self-taught architect Friedensreich Hundertwasser considered this 312-room hotel/spa, built over three thermal springs, his masterpiece. Inspired by Egon Schiele, with a nod to Gaudí, the bold colours take on surreal forms as the sunlight changes. The eight Waldhofhäuser apartments are recommended. Mostly underground, light pours in via the ceiling.
T 03383 5100, www.blumau.com

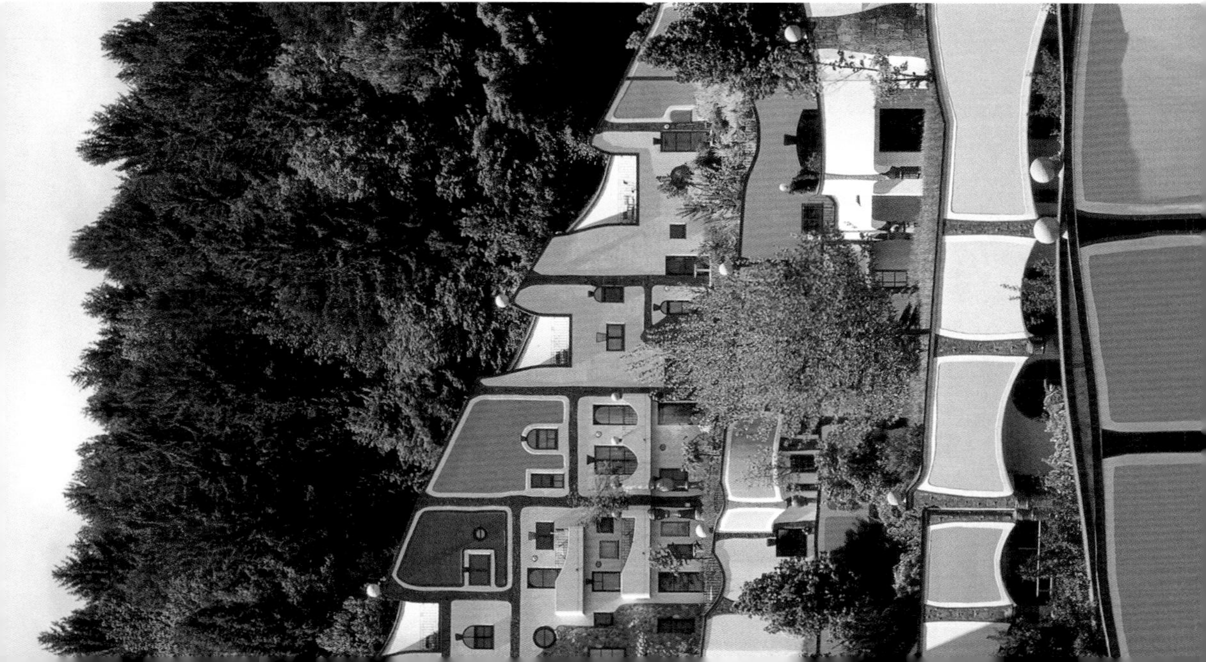

NOTES
SKETCHES AND MEMOS

RESOURCES

CITY GUIDE DIRECTORY

HOTELS

ADDRESSES AND ROOM RATES

Altstadt 020
Room rates:
double, €129-€159;
Matteo Thun rooms, €159-€189;
Matteo Thun Suite, €299
Kirchengasse 41
T 522 6666
www.altstadt.at

Das Triest 016
Room rates:
double, €258
Wiedner Hauptstraße 12
T 589 180

Do & Co Hotel 031
Room rates:
double, €280-€430;
Suite 400, €740
Stephansplatz 12
T 24 188
www.doco.com

Hollmann Beletage 016
Room rates:
double, €130-€170
Köllnerhofgasse 6
T 961 1960
www.hollmann-beletage.at

Hotel Bristol 022
Room rates:
double, €525;
Prince of Wales Suite, €4,275
Kärntner Ring 1
T 515 160
www.westin.com/bristol

Hotel Imperial 016
Room rates:
double, €724-€824
Kärntner Ring 16
T 501 100
www.starwoodhotels.com

Hotel Rathaus
Wein & Design 028
Room rates:
double, €148-€198;
Room 404, €148-€198
Lange Gasse 13
T 400 1122
www.hotel-rathaus-wien.at

Hotel Sacher 016
Room rates:
double, €350-€5,000
Philharmonikerstraße 4
T 514 560
www.sacher.com

The Levante Parliament 026
Room rates:
double, €260;
Junior Suite, €320
Auerspergstraße 15
T 535 4515
www.thelevante.com

Le Méridien 024
Room rates:
double, €215-€355
Opernring 13
T 588 900
www.lemeridien.com

Palais Coburg 017
Room rates:
double, from €500;
Modern Suite, from €1,130;
Victoria Imperial Blue Suite, €1,920
Coburgbastei 4
T 518 180
www.palais-coburg.com

Style Hotel 030
Room rates:
double, €178-€218
Hèrrengasse 12
T 227 800
www.stylehotel.at

WALLPAPER* CITY GUIDES

Editorial Director
Richard Cook

Art Director
Loran Stosskopf
City Editor
Paul Sentobe
Project Editor
Rachael Moloney
Executive Managing Editor
Jessica Firmin

Chief Designer
Ben Blossom
Designer
Ingvild Sandal

Map Illustrator
Russell Bell

Photography Editor
Christopher Lands
Photography Assistant
Jasmine Labeau

Chief Sub-Editor
Jeremy Case
Sub-Editor
Sue Delaney
Assistant Sub-Editor
Milly Nolan

Wallpaper* Group Editor-in-Chief
Tony Chambers
Publishing Director
Gord Ray
Publisher
Neil Sumner

Contributors
Paul Barnes
Jeroen Bergmans
Alan Fletcher
Sara Henrichs
David McKendrick
Claudia Perin
Meirion Pritchard
James Reid
Ellie Stathaki

Wallpaper* ® is a
registered trademark
of IPC Media Limited

All prices are correct at
time of going to press,
but are subject to change.

PHAIDON

Phaidon Press Limited
Regent's Wharf
All Saints Street
London N1 9PA

Phaidon Press Inc
180 Varick Street
New York, NY 10014

Phaidon® is a registered
trademark of Phaidon
Press Limited

www.phaidon.com

First published 2007
Reprinted 2008
© 2007 IPC Media Limited

ISBN 978 0 7148 4734 4

A CIP Catalogue record
for this book is available
from the British Library.

All rights reserved.
No part of this publication
may be reproduced,
stored in a retrieval system
or transmitted, in any
form or by any means,
electronic, mechanical,
photocopying, recording
or otherwise, without
the prior permission of
Phaidon Press.

Printed in China

PHOTOGRAPHERS

Claudio Alessandri
Palais Coburg, p017

Anne Blau
Österreicher im MAK, p041

Oliver Gast
T-Center, pp014-015
Hochhaus Neue Donau,
p065
Christus Hoffnung der
Welt, pp066-067
Church of the Most Holy
Trinity, pp070-071
Amalienbad, pp092-093

Getty Images
Vienna city view, inside
front cover

**Christian Hager/
Keystone**
Vienna International
Centre, pp010-011

Nicolas Lackner
Kunsthaus, Graz,
pp098-099

Margherita Spillutini
Ernst-Happel-Stadion,
pp094-095

**Jerzy Surwillo/Studio
Hollein**
Schullin, p037

Gerald Zugmann
Österreichische
Postsparkasse, p012
Transformer Station, p013
Café-Restaurant 'UNA', p033
MAK, p036
Kleines Café, p045
Yellow, pp046-047
Loos American Bar,
pp050-051
Ra'Mien, pp052-053
Volksgarten, pp054-055
Planter's Club, p058
Fabios, p059
Passage, pp060-061
Felix Muhrhofer, p063
Gasometer, p068, p069
Park, pp076-077
Song, p080
Unger und Klein,
pp082-083
Michél Mayer, p084
Brillen.manufaktur, p085
Rauminhalt, pp086-087
Krieau, pp090-091

Franz Zwickl
Stadtbild room, Palais
Coburg, pp018-019

VIENNA
A COLOUR-CODED GUIDE TO THE HOT 'HOODS

DONAUSTADT
Skyscrapers jostle for position on this island in the Danube, Vienna's Canary Wharf

LEOPOLDSTADT
A proposed metro extension has led to gentrification of this historic, park-filled quarter

MUSEUMSQUARTIER
This contemporary cultural centre is an urban success story, boasting daring new builds

FREIHAUSVIERTEL
Boutiques, design shops and fin-de-siècle apartments centre around Schleifmühlgasse

NEUBAU AND SPITTELBERG
A real hotchpotch of avant-garde boutiques, residential streets, cafés and corner pubs

INNERE STADT
The city centre is a World Heritage Site with a mix of baroque and modernist architecture

For a full description of each neighbourhood, see the Introduction.
Featured venues are colour-coded, according to the district in which they are located.